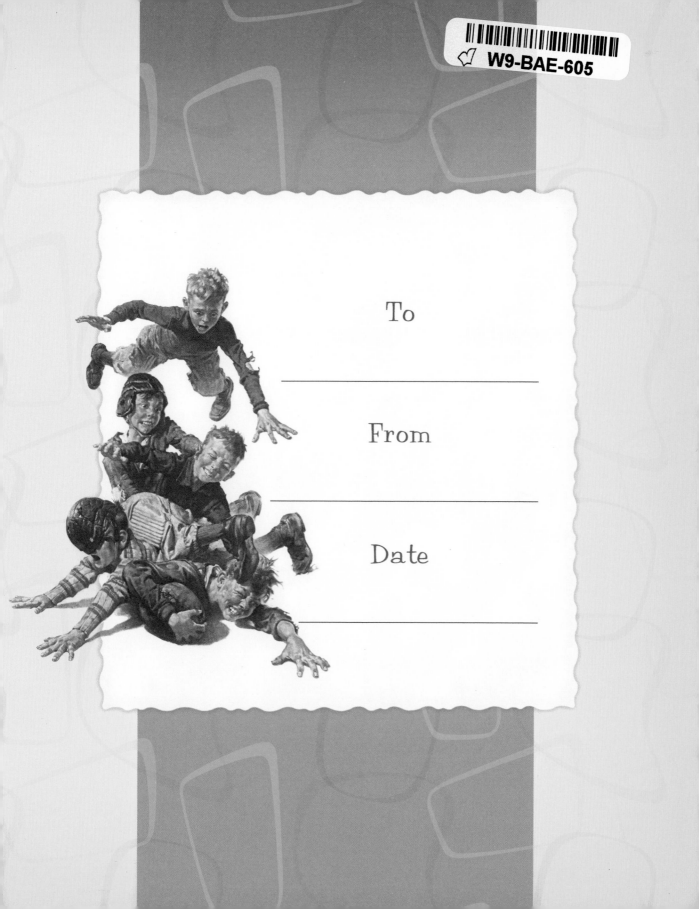

To

_____

From

_____

Date

_____

THE SATURDAY
EVENING POST

Grandpa's Memories of Growing Up

A Keepsake Record Book

HARVEST HOUSE PUBLISHERS

EUGENE, OREGON

Cover and Interior Design by Garborg Design Works, Savage, Minnesota

All illustrations © SEPS. Licensed by Curtis Licensing, Indianapolis, IN. All Rights Reserved.

Harvest House Publishers has made every effort to trace the ownership of all poems and quotes. In the event of a question arising from the use of a poem or quote, we regret any error made and will be pleased to make the necessary correction in future editions of this book.

Grandpa's Memories of Growing Up

Published by Harvest House Publishers
Eugene, Oregon 97402
www.harvesthousepublishers.com

ISBN 978-0-7369-2983-7

Printed in China

11 12 13 14 15 16 17 18 19 / LP / 10 9 8 7 6 5 4 3 2 1

This memory book is created by

_____

with love for

_____

The heart hath its own memory, like the mind,
And in it are enshrined
The precious keepsakes, into which is wrought
The giver's loving thought.

HENRY WADSWORTH LONGFELLOW

Your Arrival

When and where were you born?_____

_____

_____

Who was there to welcome you to the world?_____

_____

_____

_____

What is your full name?_____

_____

Did you have a nickname as a kid? _____

_____

Share a story you've heard about your birth. _____

_____

_____

_____

_____

Heaven lies about us in our infancy.

WILLIAM WORDSWORTH

Those who loved you and were helped by you will remember you when forget-me-nots have withered. Carve your name on hearts, not on marble.

CHARLES H. SPURGEON

Family Story

Who were your parents and where were they from?_____
_____
_____

Were you an only child or did you have siblings?_____
_____
_____

Where does your family originate from?_____
_____
_____
_____
_____

A happy family is but
an earlier heaven.

Sir John Bowring

6

What is something special or unique about your family's past or present?_____

_____

_____

_____

_____

_____

_____

_____

_____

_____

_____

_____

_____

_____

_____

_____

Our home joys are the most delightful earth affords, and the joy of parents in their children is the most holy joy of humanity. It makes their hearts pure and good, it lifts men up to their Father in heaven.

JOHANN PESTALOZZI

Introduce Yourself

Describe your personality as a kid._____

_____

_____

_____

_____

_____

_____

What significant events in history were going on during your childhood?_____

_____

_____

_____

_____

What ideas, people, or beliefs shaped your view of life as a child?_____

_____

_____

_____

Every child born into the world is a new thought
of God, an ever-fresh and radiant possibility.

KATE DOUGLAS WIGGIN

Share a fun memory of your early years. _____

A good heart, benevolent feelings, and a balanced mind, lie at the foundation of character.

JOHN TODD

Best Buds

Who have been your closest friends over the years, and what do you love about them? _____

_____

_____

_____

_____

_____

What was your favorite activity to do with friends?

_____

_____

_____

_____

*Every house where love abides
and friendship is a guest, is surely
home, and home, sweet home;
for there the heart can rest.*

Henry Van Dyke

_____

_____

Share a story about time spent with your pals._____

_____

_____

_____

_____

_____

_____

What qualities do you think make the best kind of friend?_____

_____

_____

_____

_____

_____

_____

_____

_____

Of all the things which
wisdom provides to
make life entirely happy,
much the greatest is the
possession of friendship.

EPICURUS

Pet Pals

What pets have you had during your life?_____

_____

_____

_____

_____

Which was your favorite?_____

_____

_____

_____

_____

_____

_____

_____

_____

Stay is a charming word
in a friend's vocabulary.

AMOS BRONSON ALCOTT

Was there an animal you always

wanted but never got to have? _____

_____

_____

_____

_____

_____

_____

Did you have an adventure with an animal pal? _____

_____

_____

_____

_____

_____

_____

_____

_____

There is only one happiness in life, to love and be loved.

GEORGE SAND

Readin' and Writin'

What were your favorite/least favorite subjects in school?_____

_____

_____

_____

_____

Which activities outside of the classroom were your favorites? Sports? Clubs? _____

_____

_____

_____

_____

_____

_____

_____

_____

Children have more need
of models than of critics.

JOSEPH JOUBERT

What did you love about your school or school days? _____

_____

_____

_____

_____

_____

How did a teacher or mentor make

a difference in your life? _____

_____

_____

_____

_____

_____

_____

_____

_____

_____   *To make knowledge valuable, you must have the*
cheerfulness of wisdom. Goodness smiles to the last.

_____   RALPH WALDO EMERSON

Teen Life

What clothes and music were popular when you were a teen? _____
_____
_____
_____

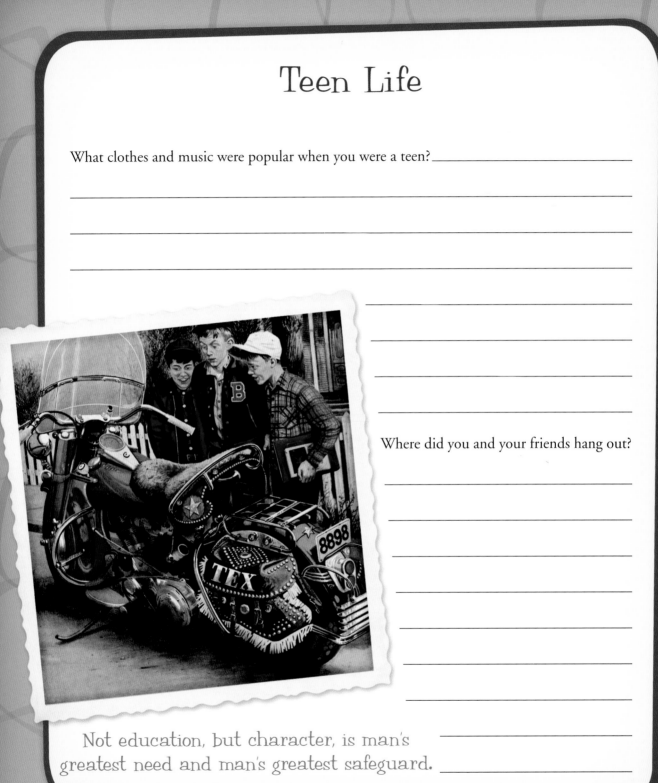

Where did you and your friends hang out?

_____
_____
_____
_____
_____
_____

Not education, but character, is man's
greatest need and man's greatest safeguard.

SPENCER

16

What kind of car did you first drive?_____

_____

_____

_____

_____

_____

_____

Every time a man smiles,
and much more when he
laughs, it adds something
to his fragment of life.

LAURENCE STERNE

Share a story about your life as a teenager._____

_____

_____

_____

_____

_____

_____

_____

_____

_____

_____

Run, Jump, and Play

What were your favorite games to play as a child? _____

_____

_____

_____

_____

_____

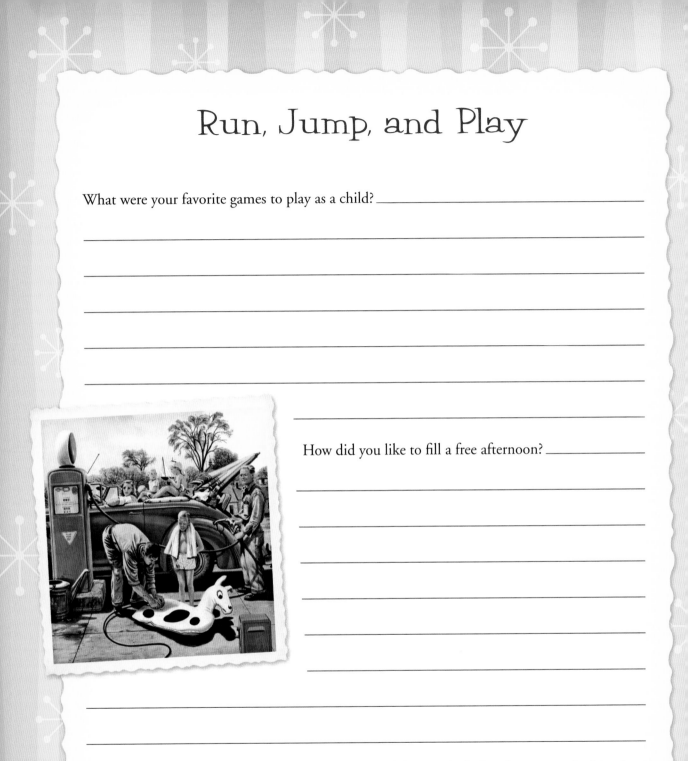

How did you like to fill a free afternoon? _____

_____

_____

_____

_____

_____

_____

_____

_____

The joys I have possessed are ever mine; out of thy reach, behind eternity, hid in the
sacred treasure of the past, but blest remembrance brings them hourly back.

JOHN DRYDEN

What game or activity do you want to share with your grandchild? _____

_____

_____

_____

_____

_____

_____

_____

_____

_____

_____

_____

_____

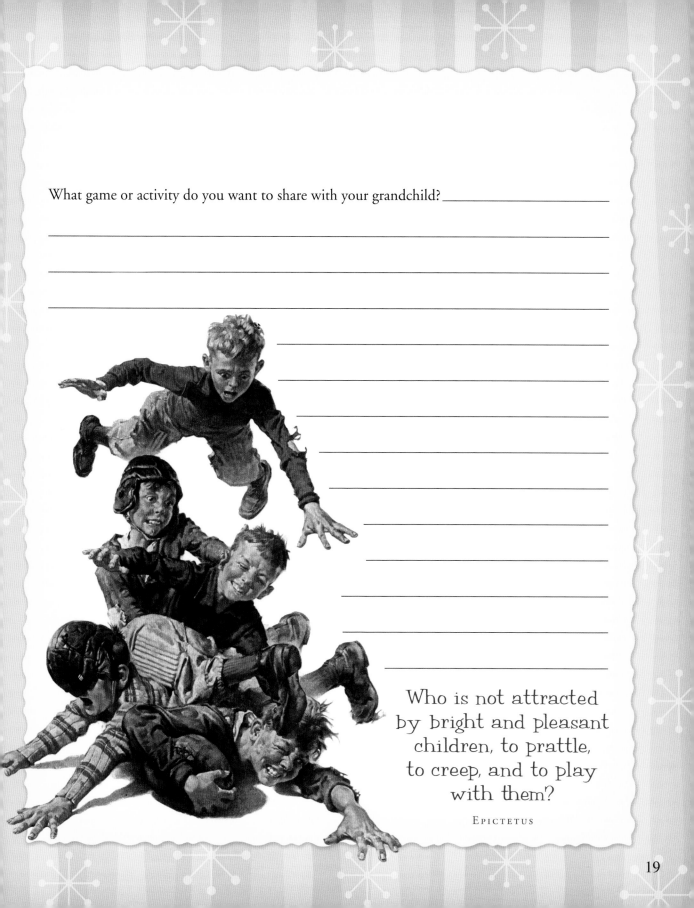

Who is not attracted
by bright and pleasant
children, to prattle,
to creep, and to play
with them?

EPICTETUS

19

Outdoor Wonders

When you were in the great outdoors as a kid, what did you love to do? Swim, hike, hunt?

_____

_____

_____

_____

_____

_____

Describe your favorite places in creation then and now. _____

_____

_____

_____

_____

_____

_____

_____

Everybody needs beauty as well as bread, places to play in and pray in, where nature may heal and give strength to body and soul.

JOHN MUIR

Who introduced you to a special outdoor activity?

What was it? _____

_____

_____

_____

_____

_____

Share a memory about enjoying nature as a boy.

_____

_____

_____

The fairest flower in the garden of creation is a young mind, offering and unfolding itself to the influence of the divine wisdom, as the heliotrope turns its sweet blossoms to the sun.

JAMES EDWARD SMITH

_____

_____

_____

_____

Creative Notions

Tell me about something you made or created. _____

_____

_____

_____

_____

What were your favorite books to read? _____

_____

_____

_____

_____

_____

_____

_____

The plays of natural lively children are the infancy of art.
Children live in a world of imagination and feeling. They
invest the most insignificant object with any form they
please, and see in it whatever they wish to see.

ADAM OEHLENSCHLAGER

How did you like to express yourself as a child?_____

_____

_____

_____

_____

_____

Describe your favorite hobbies as a kid and now. _____

_____

_____

_____

_____

_____

_____

_____

_____

What we learn with
pleasure, we never forget.

ALFRED MERCIER

23

Big Dreams

What did you daydream about as a young boy? _____

_____

_____

_____

_____

_____

Who, in your life, encouraged you to dream big? _____

_____

_____

_____

_____

_____

_____

_____

Youth is the opportunity to do
something and to become somebody.

THEODORE MUNGER

Who were your heroes and why?_____

_____

_____

_____

_____

_____

_____

_____

_____

_____

*Youth is the gay and pleasant
spring of life, when joy is stirring
in the dancing blood, and nature
calls us with a thousand songs to
share her general feast.*

Joseph Ridgeway

What goal did you work hard to achieve?_____

_____

_____

_____

_____

_____

_____

Spirit of Adventure

What was your biggest adventure as a kid?

_____

_____

_____

_____

_____

_____

_____

What adventure do you still want to enjoy?

_____

_____

_____

_____

*Children and genius have the
same master-organ in common—
inquisitiveness. Let childhood have
its way, and as it began where genius
begins it may find what genius finds.*

EDWARD BULWER-LYTTON

_____

_____

_____

Describe a time when your curiosity got you in trouble or led to an adventure.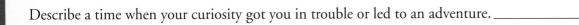

_____

_____

_____

_____

_____

If you could take your grandchildren on one great adventure, what would that adventure look like?

_____

_____

_____

_____

_____

_____

Curiosity is as much the parent of
attention, as attention is of memory.

RICHARD WHATELY

Hometown Memories

What did you love about your hometown? _____

_____

_____

_____

_____

Describe your childhood house, room, yard, and neighborhood. _____

_____

_Home is the resort of love, of joy, of peace, and plenty, where supporting
and supported, polished friends and dearest relatives mingle into bliss._

JAMES THOMSON

What was your first home as an adult like? _____

_____

_____ Childhood shows the man,
as morning shows the day.

_____

_____

_____

_____

If you could choose to live anywhere in the world,

where would it be? _____

_____

_____

_____

_____

_____

_____

_____

Favorite Traditions

Share a mealtime prayer or tradition you remember from childhood. _____

_____

_____

_____

_____

What was the conversation about at your childhood dinner table? _____

_____

_____

_____

_____

A dining room table with children's eager, hungry faces around it,
ceases to be a mere dining room table, and becomes an altar.

SIMEON STRUNSKY

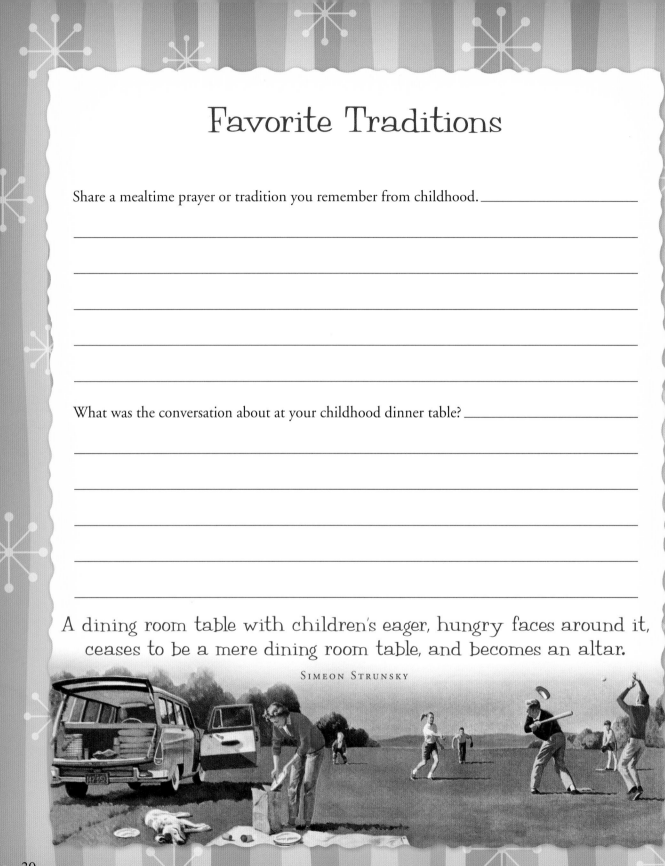

What did your family do to celebrate holidays and birthdays? _____

_____

_____

_____

Describe a memory of spending quality time

with your dad or mom. _____

_____

_____

_____

_____

_____

_____

_____

_____

_____

_____

_____

Someone says, "Boys will be boys"; he forgot to add, "Boys will be men." The future destiny of the child is always the work of the mother.

NAPOLEON BONAPARTE

The Good Life

Why are you glad that you grew up when you did?_____

_____

_____

_____

_____

_____

What made your family, community, and the country special when you were young?_____

_____

_____

_____

_____

_____

_____

What the best and wisest
parent wants for his own child
that must the community
want for all its children.

JOHN DEWEY

_____

_____

_____

_____

_____

_____

List values that will help your

grandchild create a good life._____

_____

_____

_____

_____

*The cheerful live longest in years, and
afterwards in our regards. Cheerfulness
is the off-shoot of goodness.*

CHRISTIAN NESTELL BOVEE

_____

_____

_____

_____

_____

Growing Up

When did you first feel grown up? _____

_____

_____

_____

_____

What was your first job? _____

_____

_____

_____

_____

_____

_____

_____

_____

_____

_____

The great thing in this world is not so much where
we are, but in what direction we are moving.

Oliver Wendell Holmes

What did you buy with the first money you earned or saved? _____

_____

_____

_____

Describe one of the biggest decisions you ever had to make. _____

_____

_____

_____

_____

_____

_____

_____

_____

_____

There is always one
moment in childhood
when the door opens and
lets the future in.

GRAHAM GREENE

Heart Matters

Who modeled love for you when you were young? _____

_____

_____

When did you know you were in love? _____

_____

_____

_____

_____

What do you remember most about your wedding day? _____

_____

_____

_____

_____

*You will find as you look back upon life
that the moments when you have really
lived are the moments when you have
done things in the spirit of love.*

HENRY DRUMMOND

The sweetest roamer is
a boy's young heart.

GEORGE EDWARD WOODBERRY

_____

_____

_____

_____

_____

_____

_____

Share something you've learned about loving and caring for others._____

_____

_____

_____

_____

_____

_____

_____

_____

_____

Faith and Joy

When did you experience the deepest sense of joy as a child? _____

_____

_____

_____

_____

_____

_____

_____

_____

Where did you feel safest or the closest to God? _____

_____

_____

_____

_____

_____

In the man whose childhood has known caresses and kindness,
there is always a fiber of memory that can be touched to gentle issues.

GEORGE ELIOT

What inspires your faith and sense

of hope now? _____

_____

_____

_____

_____

_____

_____

_____

Faith is the root of all blessings.

JEREMY TAYLOR

_____

_____

_____

_____

_____

_____

_____

_____

_____

Memories and Legacies

Do you have a special memory of your grandparents? _____

_____

_____

_____

What character traits do you get from your parents? _____

_____

_____

_____

_____

_____

_____

_____

_____

_____

There is a magic in that little
word, home; it is a mystic
circle that surrounds comforts
and virtues never known
beyond its hallowed limits.

ROBERT SOUTHEY

There is not a man or woman, however poor they may be, but have it in their power, by the grace of God, to leave behind them the grandest thing on earth, character; and their children might rise up after them and thank God that their mother was a pious woman, or their father a pious man.

NORMAN MACLEOD

As a boy, what did you love to do with your father?

Describe your favorite family tradition or the memory of a special gathering or holiday. _____

Becoming a Parent and Grandparent

What are your fondest memories of being a parent? _____

_____

_____

_____

_____

_____

_____

_____

_____

_____

_____

_____

_____

_____

_____

God sends children for another purpose than merely to keep up the race—to enlarge our hearts; and to make us unselfish and full of kindly sympathies and affections; to give our souls higher aims; to call out all our faculties to extended enterprise and exertion; and to bring round our firesides bright faces, happy smiles, and loving, tender hearts.

Mary Howitt

What do you see in your child or grandchild that reminds you of yourself?_____

_____

_____

_____

_____

What is the greatest joy of being a grandparent? _____

_____

_____   Grandchildren are the
crowning glory of the aged;
_____   Parents are the pride of
their children.
_____

THE BOOK OF PROVERBS

_____

_____

_____

_____

_____

A Grandparents Wisdom

Share wisdom or a life lesson that you want to pass on. _____

_____

_____

_____

_____

_____

What are life's greatest rewards? _____

_____

_____

_____

_____

_____

Pass along some words of wisdom that your parents or grandparents gave to you. _____

_____

_____

_____

The truest greatness lies in being kind, the truest wisdom in a happy mind.

Ella Wheeler Wilcox

Children are the hands by
which we take hold of heaven.

HENRY WARD BEECHER

_____

_____

_____

_____

_____

What is your biggest hope

for your grandchild?_____

_____

_____

_____

_____

_____

_____

_____

_____

_____

A Letter to Your Grandchild

What do you want your grandchildren and future generations to know about you, your family, and your childhood?_____

_____

_____

_____

_____

_____

_____

_____

_____

_____

_____

_____

_____

_____

_____

Perfect love sometimes does not come till the first grandchild.

WELSH PROVERB

Don't judge each day by the harvest you reap, but by the seeds you plant.

Robert Louis Stevenson

I have often thought what a melancholy world this would be without children; and what an inhuman world, without the aged.

SAMUEL COLERIDGE